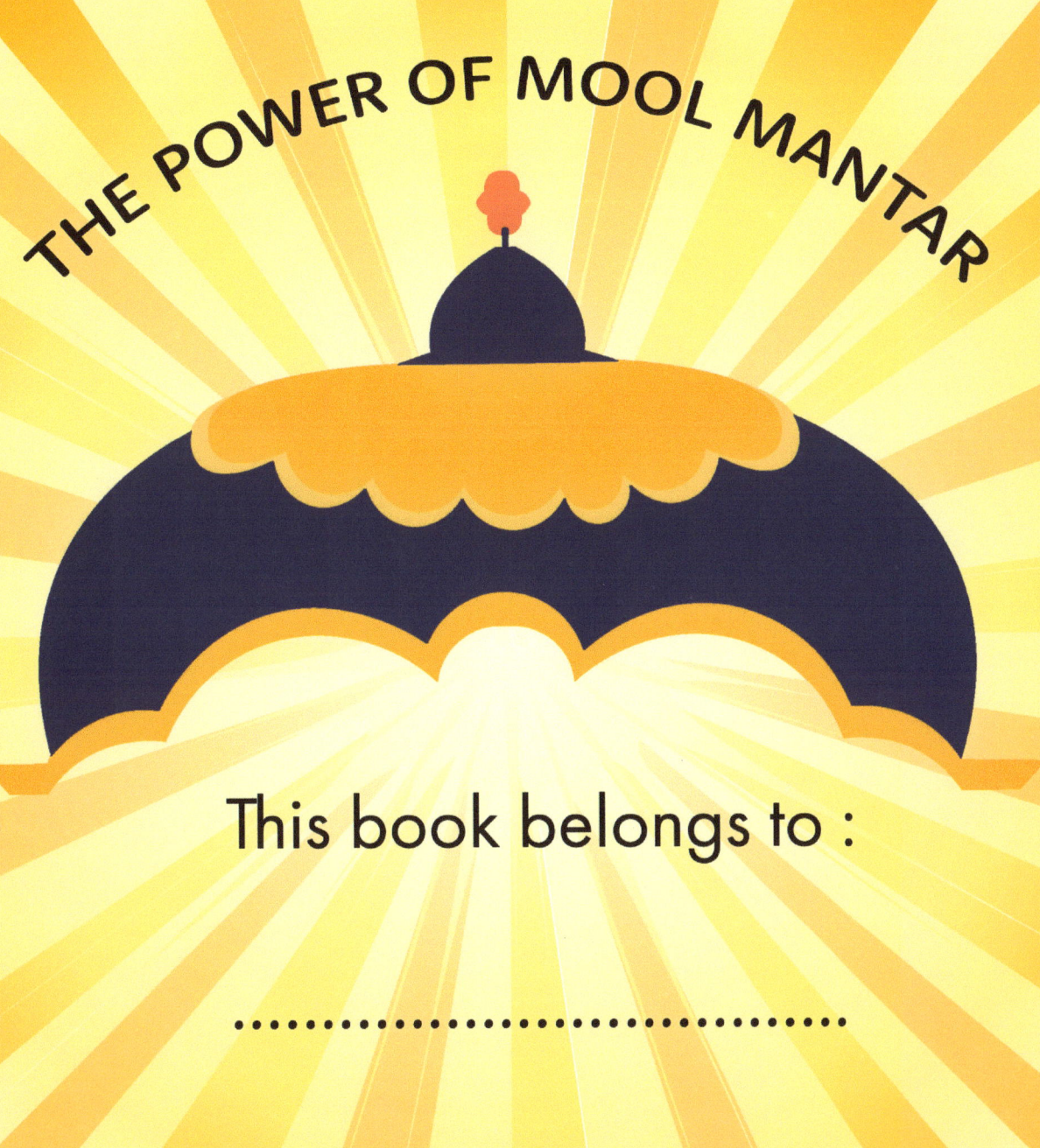

THE POWER OF MOOL MANTAR

This book belongs to :

....

....

Copyright © 2022 Little Guru Books - All rights reserved.

ISBN: 978-0-6489840-4-7 Hardback
ISBN: 978-0-6489840-3-0 Paperback
ISBN: 978-0-6489840-5-4 EPub

No part of the publication may be reproduced, stored in a retrieval system, or transmitted in any form or by any means (including electronic, mechanical, photocopying, recording, or otherwise) without prior permission of the author.

The Author and the publisher do not hold any responsibility for errors, omissions or contrary interpretation of the subject matter herein. This book is presented solely for inspirational and informational purposes only.

To my beautiful children, *Samreet* and *Ranveer*, who keep on inspiring me to make meaningful books.

THREE PILLARS OF SIKHISM

Guru Nanak Dev Ji taught us that the essence of life consists of the three pillars in Sikhism:

- **Naam Japna** - keeping Waheguru in mind at all times
- **Kirat Karna** - earning an honest living
- **Vand Chhakna** - sharing and caring for others

WHO IS WAHEGURU?

Waheguru is a Gurmukhi word meaning the "Wonderful Lord". In the Guru Granth Sahib - the holy book of Sikhs, Waheguru directly refers to God. In Sikhism, you might hear many names being used to refer to God, for example, Waheguru, Satnaam, Ik Onkar, Akal Purakh and so on. In Gurbani using the word Waheguru helps us connect with God. Chanting and meditating on his name clears our hearts and minds.

WHAT IS GURBANI?

Gurbani refers to the holy scriptures of the Sikh Gurus. These scriptures can be found in the Guru Granth Sahib - the holy book for Sikhs. Gurbani is composed of two words : 'Guru' and 'Bani'. The word 'Guru' refers to the spiritual teacher and 'Bani' refers to the teachings of the Gurus. Japji Sahib is the first Bani found at the beginning of the Guru Granth Sahib. Japji Sahib begins with a short section called Mool Mantar.

WHAT IS MOOL MANTAR?

Mool Mantar is the first verse in the Guru Granth Sahib. It consists of words from the Punjabi language, Gurmukhi. "Mool Mantar" means the "main chant" or the "root verse". Mool Mantar encapsulates the entire spiritual essence of Sikhism.

WHO WROTE MOOL MANTAR?

Mool Mantar is the first composition of Guru Nanak Dev Ji, the founder of Sikhism. It is also the first verse of the Guru Granth Sahib. Guru Nanak Dev Ji defines God as timeless, formless, and an unbounded energy over space and time. He taught us that human beings have direct access to Waheguru as he lives within all of us.

WHY IS MOOL MANTAR IMPORTANT?

Mool Mantar is the most important composition in Sikhism as it summarizes the essential teachings of Guru Nanak Dev Ji. The Symbol ੴ 'Ik Onkar', the first words of the Mool Mantar, emphasize that there is only "One God". The symbol helps Sikhs to focus on Waheguru when praying and meditating.

Let us now read together...

Ik Onkar

There is only one God

ਸਤਿਨਾਮੁ

Satnaam

Eternal truth is his name

ਕਰਤਾ ਪੁਰਖੁ

Karta Purakh

He is the creator

ਨਿਰਭਉ

Nirbhau

He is without fear

ਨਿਰਵੈਰੁ

Nirvair

He is without hate

ਅਕਾਲ ਮੂਰਤਿ

Akaal Moorat

He is timeless and without form

ਅਜੂਨੀ

Ajooni

He is beyond birth and death

ਸੈਭੰ

Saibhang

The enlightened one

ਗੁਰਪ੍ਸਾਦਿ ॥

Gurprasaad

By the Guru's grace

॥ ਜਪੁ ॥
Jap

Meditate upon his name

ਆਦਿ ਸਚੁ
Aad Sach

He was true before the creation

ਜੁਗਾਦਿ ਸਚੁ

Jugaad Sach

He was true when ages commenced

ਹੈ ਭੀ ਸਚੁ
Hai Bhi Sach

He is true now

ਨਾਨਕ ਹੋਸੀ ਭੀ ਸਚੁ ॥੧॥

Nanak Hosi Bhi Sach

He will always be true

ੴ
Ik Onkar

ਸਤਿਨਾਮੁ	Satnaam
ਕਰਤਾ ਪੁਰਖੁ	Karta Purakh
ਨਿਰਭਉ	Nirbhau
ਨਿਰਵੈਰੁ	Nirvair
ਅਕਾਲ ਮੂਰਤਿ	Akaal Moorat
ਅਜੂਨੀ	Ajooni
ਸੈਭੰ	Saibhang
ਗੁਰਪ੍ਰਸਾਦਿ	Gurprasaad
ਜਪੁ	Jap
ਆਦਿ ਸਚੁ	Aad Sach
ਜੁਗਾਦਿ ਸਚੁ	Jugaad Sach
ਹੈ ਭੀ ਸਚੁ	Hai Bhi Sach
ਨਾਨਕ ਹੋਸੀ ਭੀ ਸਚੁ	Nanak Hosi Bhi Sach

੧ਓ
Ik Onkar

ਸਤਿਨਾਮੁ	Satnaam
ਕਰਤਾ ਪੁਰਖੁ	Karta Purakh
ਨਿਰਭਉ	Nirbhau
ਨਿਰਵੈਰੁ	Nirvair
ਅਕਾਲ ਮੂਰਤਿ	Akaal Moorat
ਅਜੂਨੀ	Ajooni
ਸੈਭੰ	Saibhang
ਗੁਰਪ੍ਰਸਾਦਿ	Gurprasaad
ਜਪੁ	Jap
ਆਦਿ ਸਚੁ	Aad Sach
ਜੁਗਾਦਿ ਸਚੁ	Jugaad Sach
ਹੈ ਭੀ ਸਚੁ	Hai Bhi Sach
ਨਾਨਕ ਹੋਸੀ ਭੀ ਸਚੁ	Nanak Hosi Bhi Sach

LITTLE **GURU** BOOKS

Thank you for your support.

For feedback and reviews
please visit Amazon.

FOLLOW US on Instagram :

LITTLEGURUBOOKS

Also availaible :

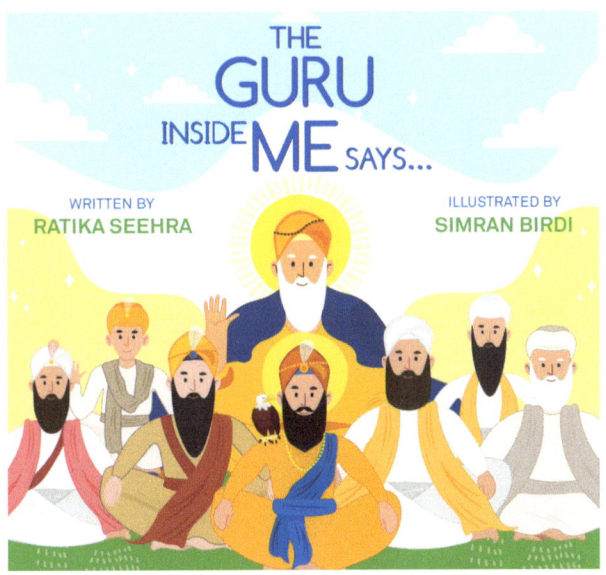

www.ingramcontent.com/pod-product-compliance
Lightning Source LLC
Chambersburg PA
CBHW040732150426
42811CB00063B/1583